Favoring a traditional
American style, President
Joseph R. Biden Jr. wears
a navy pinstripe suit with
a white shirt and blue-
and-white striped tie.

President Joseph R. Biden Jr.   PLATE 1

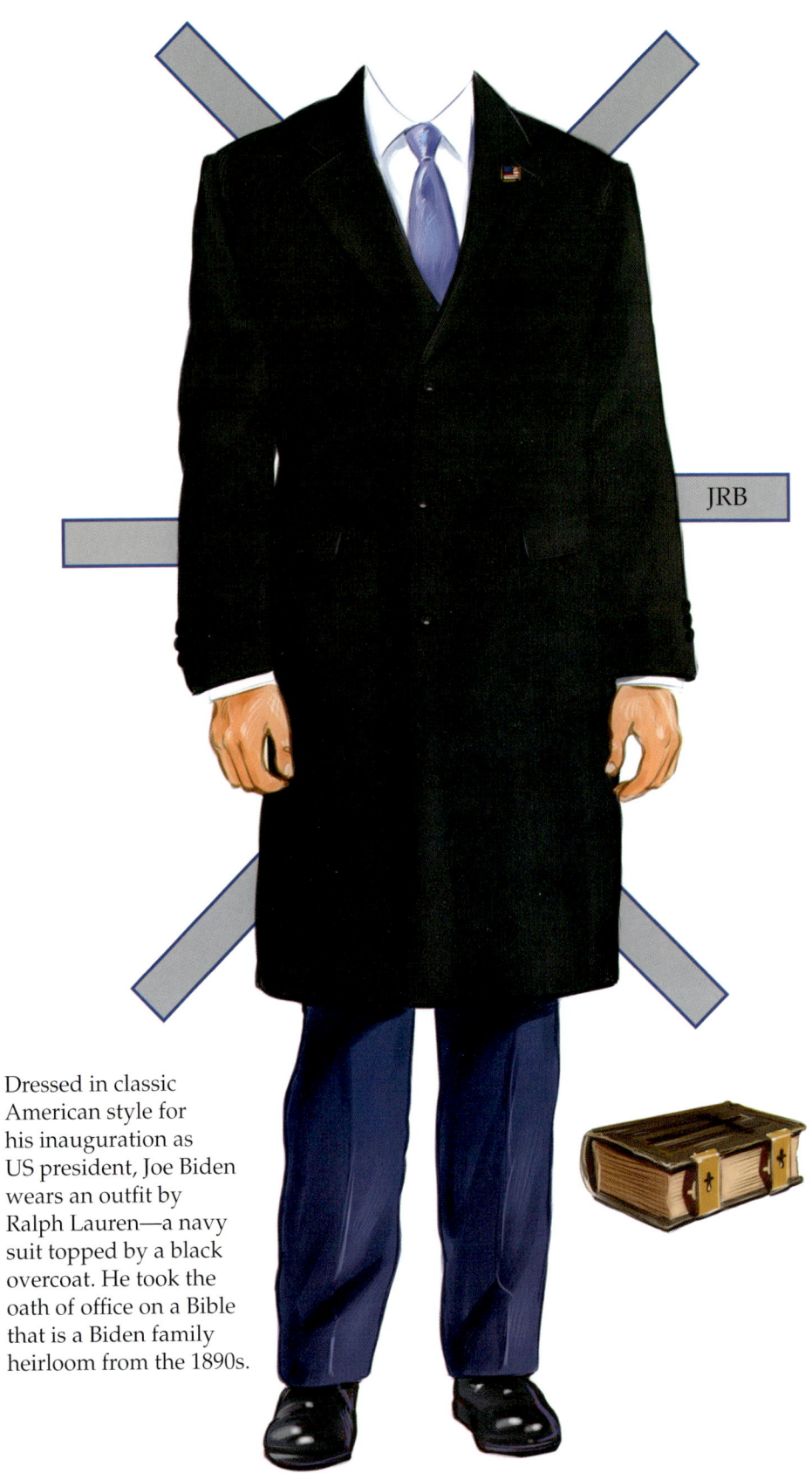

JRB

Dressed in classic American style for his inauguration as US president, Joe Biden wears an outfit by Ralph Lauren—a navy suit topped by a black overcoat. He took the oath of office on a Bible that is a Biden family heirloom from the 1890s.

PLATE 2

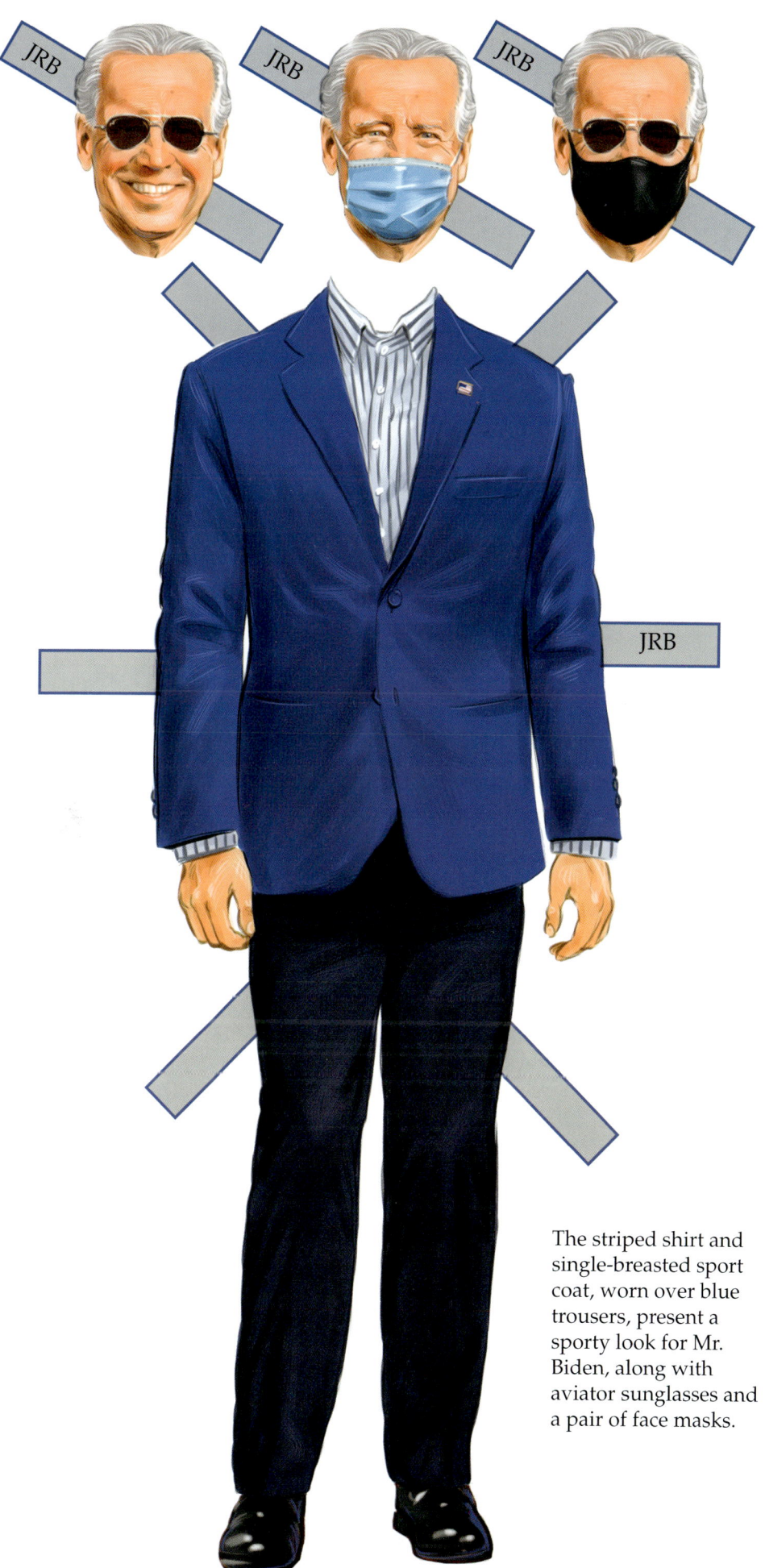

The striped shirt and single-breasted sport coat, worn over blue trousers, present a sporty look for Mr. Biden, along with aviator sunglasses and a pair of face masks.

PLATE 3

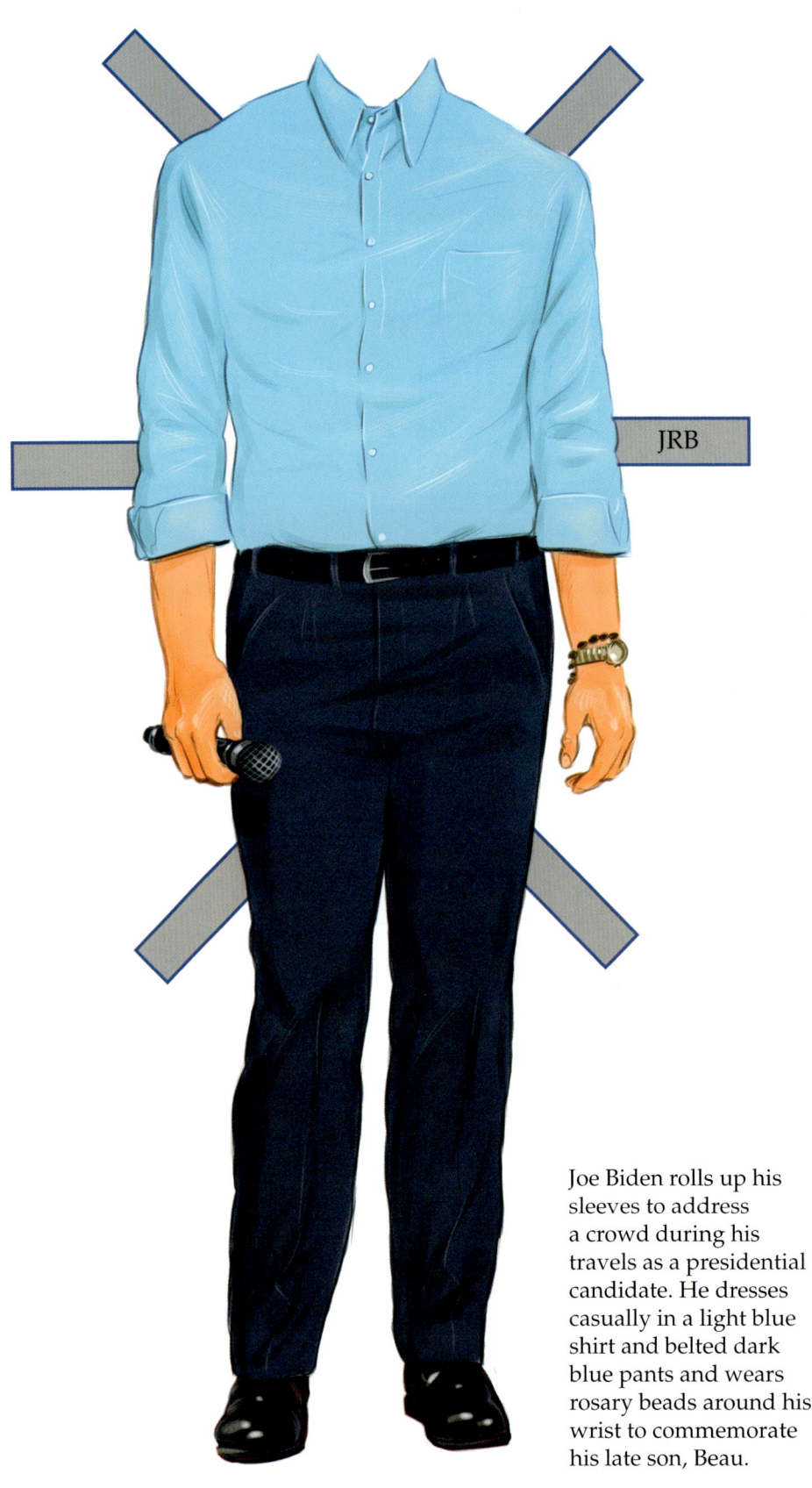

JRB

Joe Biden rolls up his sleeves to address a crowd during his travels as a presidential candidate. He dresses casually in a light blue shirt and belted dark blue pants and wears rosary beads around his wrist to commemorate his late son, Beau.

PLATE 4

Vice President Kamala Harris wears a gray single-breasted notch-collar suit jacket and coordinating skirt, along with a dark blue tie-neck blouse and black pumps.

Vice President Kamala Harris   PLATE 5

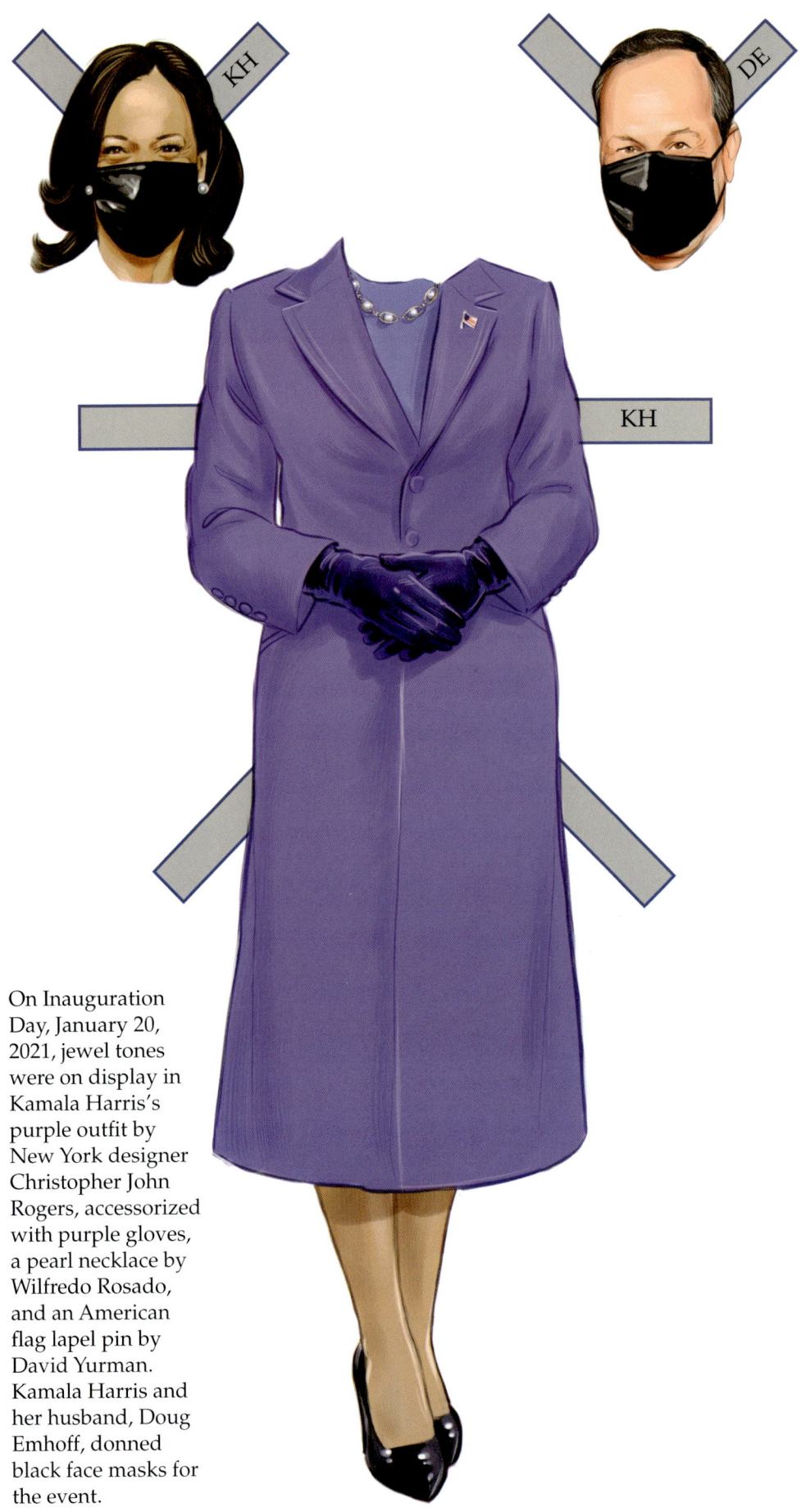

On Inauguration Day, January 20, 2021, jewel tones were on display in Kamala Harris's purple outfit by New York designer Christopher John Rogers, accessorized with purple gloves, a pearl necklace by Wilfredo Rosado, and an American flag lapel pin by David Yurman. Kamala Harris and her husband, Doug Emhoff, donned black face masks for the event.

KH

DE

KH

PLATE 6

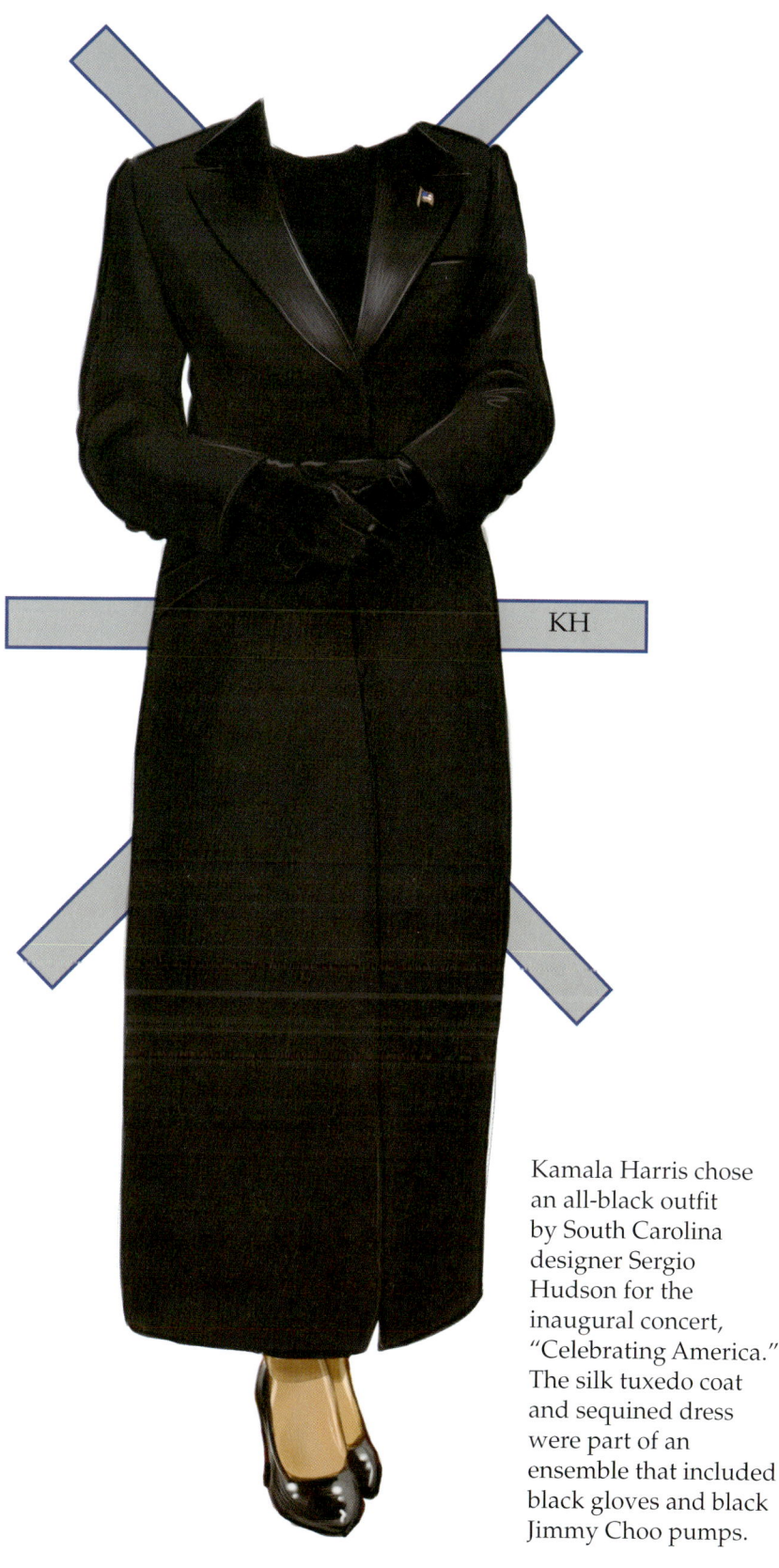

KH

Kamala Harris chose an all-black outfit by South Carolina designer Sergio Hudson for the inaugural concert, "Celebrating America." The silk tuxedo coat and sequined dress were part of an ensemble that included black gloves and black Jimmy Choo pumps.

PLATE 7

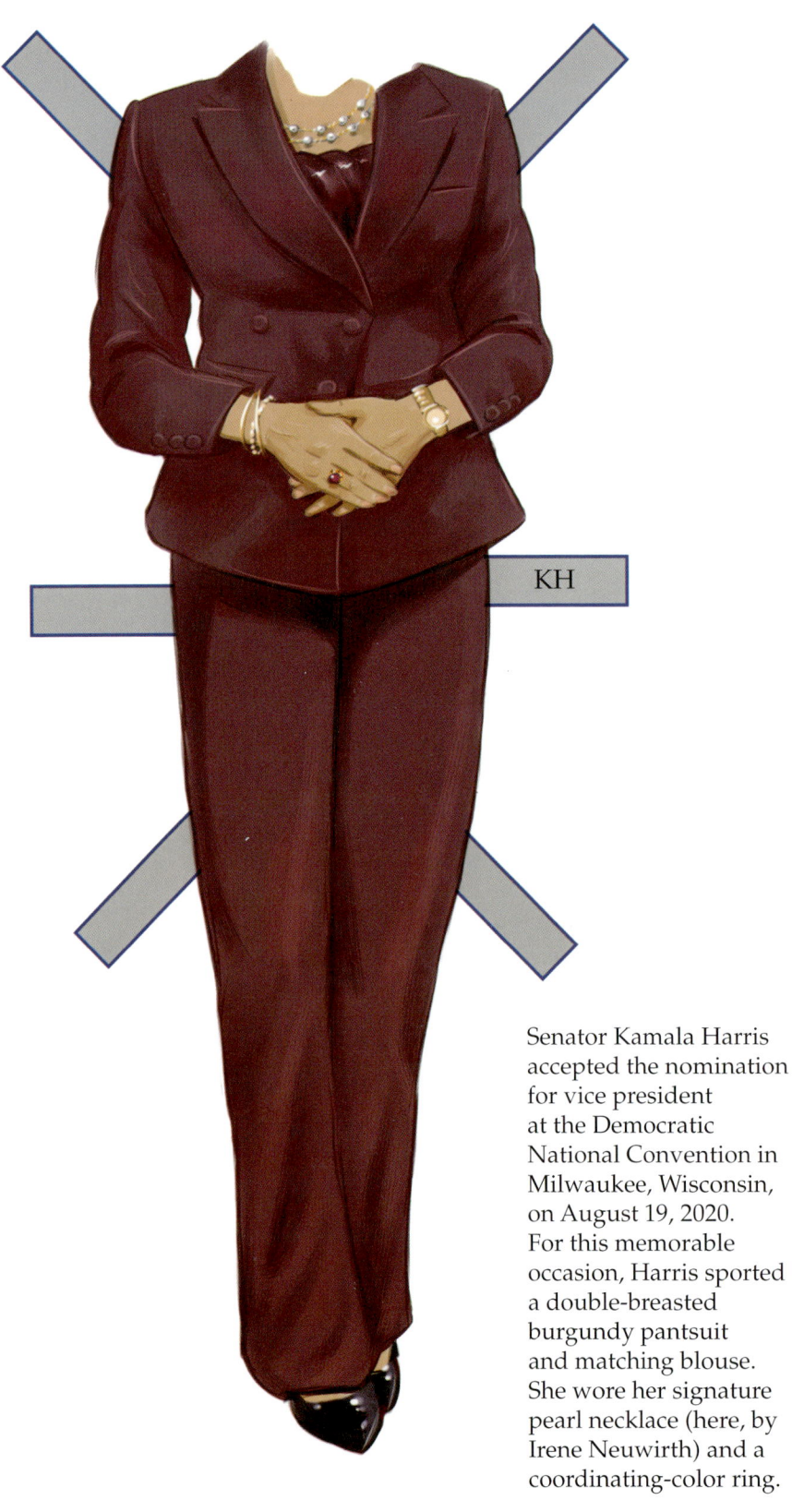

KH

Senator Kamala Harris accepted the nomination for vice president at the Democratic National Convention in Milwaukee, Wisconsin, on August 19, 2020. For this memorable occasion, Harris sported a double-breasted burgundy pantsuit and matching blouse. She wore her signature pearl necklace (here, by Irene Neuwirth) and a coordinating-color ring.

PLATE 8

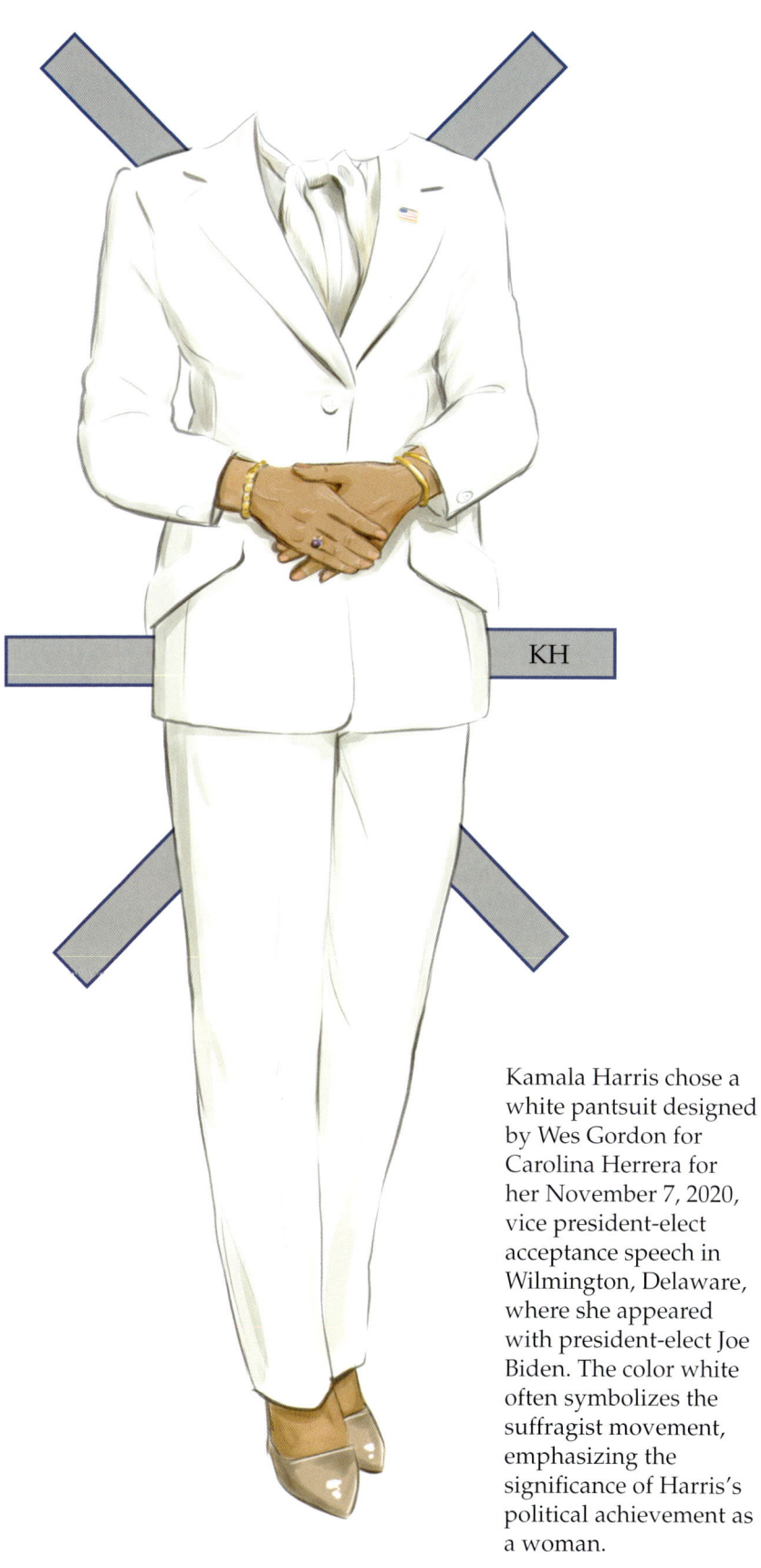

KH

Kamala Harris chose a white pantsuit designed by Wes Gordon for Carolina Herrera for her November 7, 2020, vice president-elect acceptance speech in Wilmington, Delaware, where she appeared with president-elect Joe Biden. The color white often symbolizes the suffragist movement, emphasizing the significance of Harris's political achievement as a woman.

PLATE 9

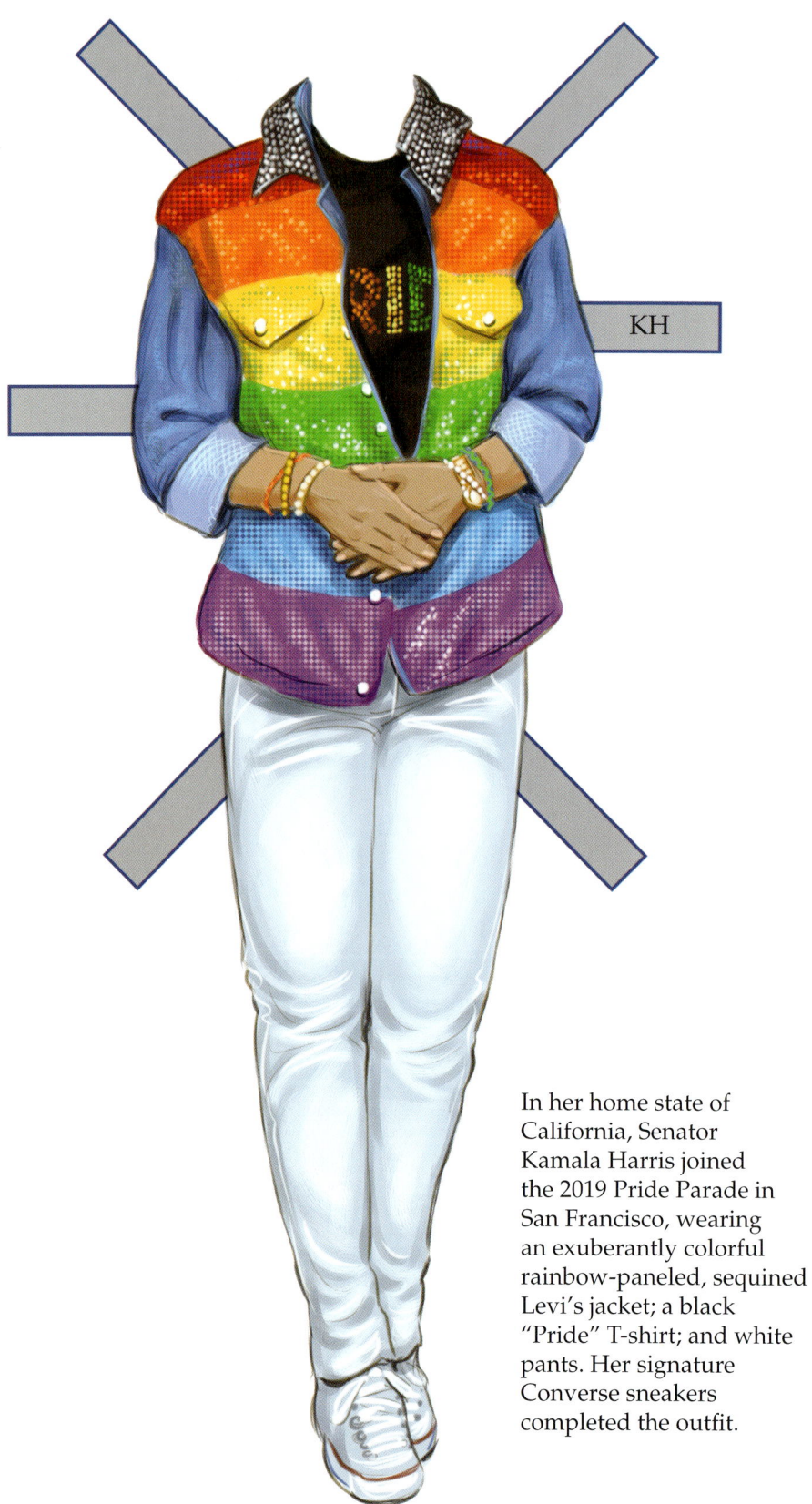

In her home state of California, Senator Kamala Harris joined the 2019 Pride Parade in San Francisco, wearing an exuberantly colorful rainbow-paneled, sequined Levi's jacket; a black "Pride" T-shirt; and white pants. Her signature Converse sneakers completed the outfit.

KH

PLATE 10

First Lady Dr. Jill Biden dresses in a French-blue knee-length, formfitting dress and matching blue heels. Dr. Biden worked as a teacher during the eight years that Joe Biden was vice president, and she plans on continuing to do so, becoming the first First Lady to remain in her professional career while her husband is in office.

First Lady Dr. Jill Biden

PLATE 11

Jill Biden wore a jewel-toned Inauguration Day outfit. Dr. Biden dressed in a sequined turquoise tweed coat and matching-color dress by Alexandra O'Neill of the New York design house Markarian, along with turquoise gloves and face mask, Monique Péan octagonal earrings, a Tyler Ellis handbag, and Jimmy Choo "Romy" pumps.

PLATE 12

The dress and double-breasted cashmere ivory coat that the First Lady wore for the inauguration's evening festivities were embroidered with flowers representing every US state and territory. The ensemble's designer is Gabriela Hearst. Desert Blooms "Mariposa" earrings are shown at the upper right.

PLATE 13

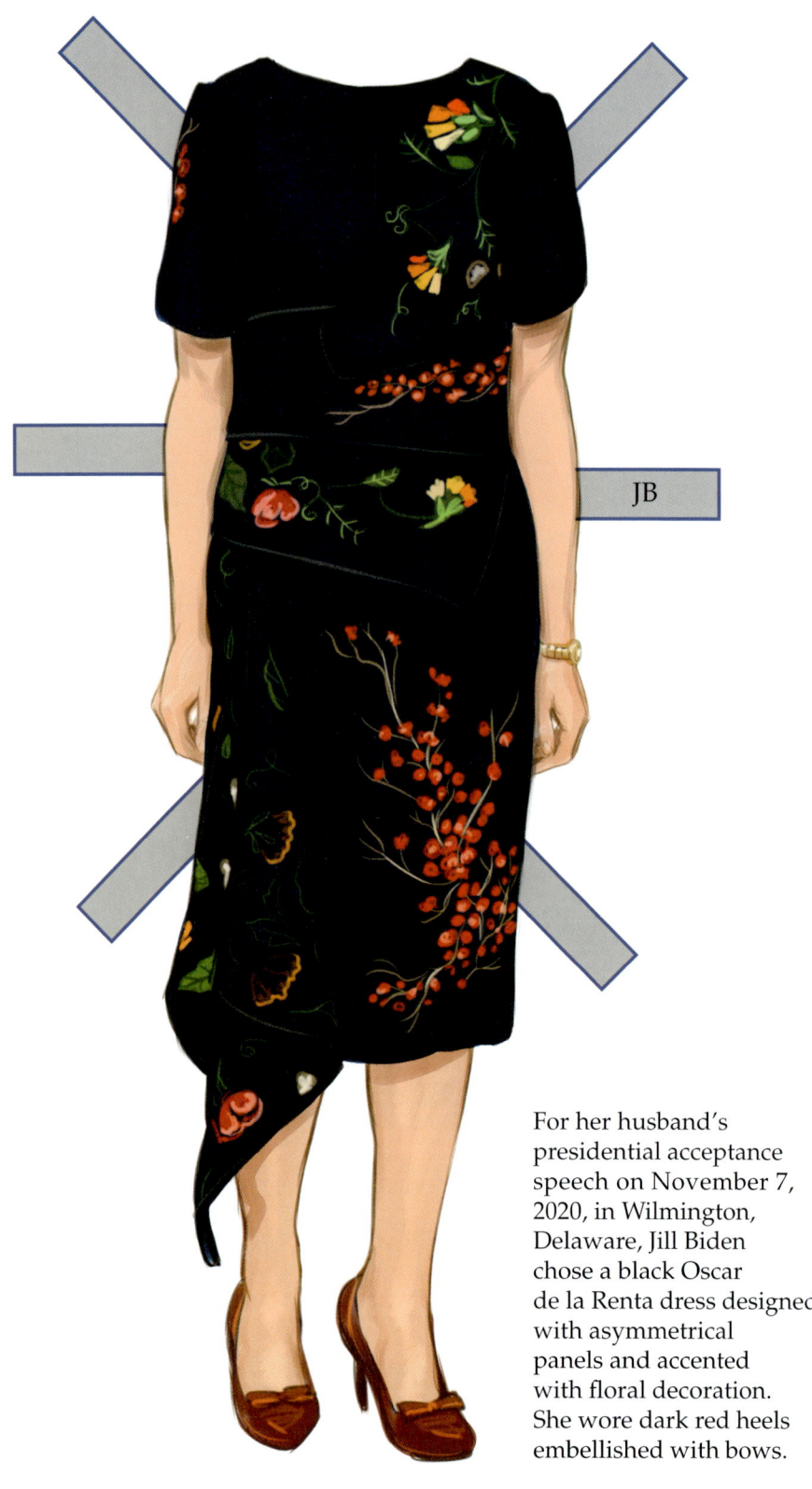

JB

For her husband's
presidential acceptance
speech on November 7,
2020, in Wilmington,
Delaware, Jill Biden
chose a black Oscar
de la Renta dress designed
with asymmetrical
panels and accented
with floral decoration.
She wore dark red heels
embellished with bows.

PLATE 14

Doug Emhoff is
dressed in a Ralph
Lauren single-breasted,
flap-pocket navy suit,
worn with a navy tie
and a light blue shirt.

Second Gentleman Douglas Emhoff   PLATE 15

The First Dogs of the Biden-Harris administration are Major (*top*) and Champ (*bottom*), both German shepherds. Major, the younger of the two, was adopted by the Bidens in 2018. Champ lived in Washington, DC, for eight years while Joe Biden was vice president.

Major

Champ

PLATE 16   *First Dogs Major and Champ*